CW00428457

I'M BORED!
IN ASSOCIATION WITH AUTAN

I'M BORED!
IN ASSOCIATION WITH AUTAN

SUZY BARRATT
AND POLLY BEARD

ILLUSTRATED BY SAM HOLLAND

BLOOMSBURY

First published 2003
This edition published in association with Autan insect repellent 2004

Copyright © Suzy Barratt and Polly Beard, 2003
Illustrations copyright © Sam Holland, 2003

The moral right of the authors has been asserted

Bloomsbury Publishing Plc, 38 Soho Square, London W1D 3HB

A CIP catalogue record for this book is available from the British Library

ISBN 07475 7689 0

Designed by Richard Horne

Printed in Italy

All papers used by Bloomsbury Publishing are natural, recyclable products
made from wood grown in well-managed forests. The manufacturing processes
conform to the environmental regulations of the country of origin.

Autan is a range of insect repellents designed to protect you and your little ones for up to eight hours, making hide-and-seek with biting insects a thing of the past.

Autan's formulation has a unique active ingredient which is highly effective against mosquitoes, midges and biting insects. Suitable for everyone over the age of two years, and with the added bonus of a fresh fragrance and a non-sticky, non-greasy application, it's every parent's best friend this summer.

Autan - tough on insects, gentle on skin

ACKNOWLEDGEMENTS

We would like to thank:

Joss and Tom for everything.

Jane Turnbull for her belief in us.

Rosemary Davidson and everyone at
Bloomsbury for their support and guidance.

Sam for her beautiful drawings.

Granny Trish and Granny Lily for their
wonderful help with our kids.

And finally, Mum, Dad and Em for
teaching us how to play in the first place.

CONTENTS

INTRODUCTION

The summer holidays mean family fun outdoors whether at home or abroad. But boredom (and the bother of biting insects!) can make everyone irritable and scratchy. With this in mind, here are loads of inspiring and imaginative ideas for creative play, to combine with the protection of Autan insect repellent for more outdoor smiles this summer.

When your children are bored and can't think of what to do next, it's often impossible to come up with an immediate and brilliant idea that will keep everyone happy. Help is at hand!

Inside this book are games we play with our own children, and others that you may be familiar with but might have forgotten how to play. Treat it as a recipe book. Dip in and out of it when you need fresh ideas and inspiration. Some of the games are short and sweet. Others may last for days on end.

There are ideas for all ages from toddlers to pre-teens. Start your kids off with any of the games – you may find that they grasp the idea quickly and play on their own, or you may be surprised to find that you want to keep playing yourself.

This book won't turn you into a 'perfect' parent or grandparent, step-parent, godparent or babysitter. But we hope that it will give you the inspiration that you sometimes need to really enjoy your time with children. And there's nothing more important than that.

So enjoy the outdoors this summer and play it safe with Autan. The range offers up to eight hours' protection against biting beasties, which means happy families for longer.

I'M BORED! ...

OUTDOORS

PICK-A-STICK

Any number of you can play this, or you can do it on your own, slowly and methodically. Collect up sticks of all different sizes and lengths – maybe twenty sticks in all, more if there are lots of you. Make sure they are all vertical, then let them fall to the ground so that they fan out and make a pile at the same time. Now take it in turns to remove a stick from the pile without any other

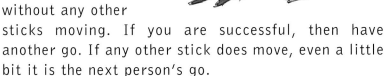

sticks moving. If you are successful, then have another go. If any other stick does move, even a little bit it is the next person's go.

    If you want to make it more difficult, you could use only your left hand if you are right-handed, or vice versa. It's also harder with gloves on. The winner is the one with the most sticks at the end, and the prize is to choose which tree to climb.

FAIRY HOUSES

These work best of all in some woods where there are plenty of sticks, leaves, moss and old trees with deep roots.

Your fairy house can be as elaborate and sophisticated and imaginative as you like. Make one in a team, or go off on your own so you'll have the freedom to do exactly as you want with it.

The key to a successful fairy house is to find the right sticks. What you need are two sturdy sticks of roughly the same length, which are forked at one end, and three more good solid sticks of a reasonable length. Choose a sheltered nook at the base of a tree in between two roots where you think the fairies might like to live. Then position your fork-shaped sticks as upright as possible with the two prongs parallel to the tree trunk. Put two more of your sturdy sticks in between the trunk and the prongs of your front forks to make the edges of the roof. It helps if you can somehow wedge these side supports into little craggy holes in the bark. Place your last sturdy stick across the front of your roof. Now all you need is a handful of twigs and sticks to form a messy criss-cross pattern on the roof. Then collect the final layer of roofing, which can be moss, bracken, grasses or leaves, and cover the roof carefully to provide an idyllic shelter.

Now comes the really fun bit, furnishing the house. Think about pieces of bark or flat stones for a table, something the fairies might like to sleep on (fairies aren't fussy if their mattresses are hard or soft), a bit of moss or leaves for bed-covers, maybe some food and plates to eat off. Acorn cups make very good wine glasses, and snail shells are excellent fruit bowls. Can you find something to become a tiny bath or a kitchen sink? Make whatever seems right for your fairy house. Don't forget a chimney. We always used to dig a little hole nearby for the fairies to use as a loo. You can also build a garden and a path in front of the house. What about a swimming pool and trees? If you have tiny children wanting to join in, it's not a bad idea to set them to work on the garden, as the houses themselves can be accidentally knocked down by less agile hands!

PEBBLE FOOTBALL ALL THE WAY HOME

This is a cracker for getting tired people to walk that tiny bit further to get you all back home, or to the car park, or wherever you are aiming for.

Any willing players should pick a stone or pebble, not so small that it is impossible to find again, and not so big that it is only going to travel a few inches every time you kick it. You want to be able to kick the stone while you are walking, without breaking your pace, and for the stone to go ahead of you by ten to twenty feet. Keep your eyes fixed on it so that you simply forget how much walking you are doing in between each kick.

It obviously helps if you are playing this game on a track or path that is gently sloping downhill, but you can still play it to help you get up a hill, although you will have to kick your pebble football many more times as it will naturally keep rolling back towards you.

LADYBIRD GARDENS

These are really good fun to make, but quite fiddly. Be prepared to get earthy fingers, and to give up a few flowers from the garden. If you are making a ladybird garden in the fields and meadows, be careful not to pick too many precious wild flowers. Ladybird gardens are harder to make in the park, but you could give it a go if there are lots of daisies. It works best if you are in the garden, where you are allowed to pick a few petals or flowers, and have access to a couple of things from indoors.

You can start off in two ways. Either find a flattish container – a seed tray is perfect if you have one, otherwise, any container with low sides, like a serving dish, or a shallow-sided cardboard box, will do. Or, if you are nowhere near a container to make it all in, you could clear a little area of the ground, and put some sticks to mark out the boundary fence, or stones to make a wall.

Fill your container with earth from the garden, or sand from the sandpit, and pat it down smoothly. Then use some small stones to make a winding path, some little leaves and flowers to make bushes and plants. See if you can make a tree out of a twig with some leaves on, or use a bit of moss to look like foliage. One of the best features in our ladybird garden was a pond, made from a pot or lid sunk into the soil, lined with tinfoil and then filled with a little water. We used to float a petal on it to look like a water lily. Can you make some garden furniture? Try using a peice of bark as a bench or table, and some snail shells as chairs. Do the ladybirds need a little vegetable garden? With a spade and a fork? If you are feeling very clever you could work out how to make a swing or a hammock. Or make a nice finish to it by making a gate or a little arch as an entrance.

TOP TIPS: 1) Make sure everyone knows which flowers and leaves are OK to pick, as some are poisonous, and some are stingers.

2) Watch out that cats don't mistake the beautiful ladybird garden for a litter tray and use it as a loo!

WALKIE TALKIE

Walks. Why can it be almost impossible to get a capable, energetic six-year-old to go that final hundred yards to the car park? Or seemingly  able-bodied eleven-year-olds willingly to join in a family ramble through the woods? Our children sometimes used to feel that walks were a chore to be endured, occasionally rewarded at the end with a packet of crisps and a fizzy drink in a pub car park. Until we all invented Walkie Talkie.

This is a magical way to keep everyone's interest going for as long as you need to, and used to make us squeal with laughter. Grandparents are especially good at this, as you can never be quite sure if they are telling the truth.

All you have to do is ask questions. You can ask anyone anything. It's really up to you whether you tell the whole truth, or whether you make up a fantastical response. The key to the game is to be informative and imaginative. There are no material prizes in this game, but you do get a lovely feeling while you are munching your pork scratchings at the pub if you think that you've found out something new and useful.

Here are some questions for children to ask adults:

- Did you like school? What were you good at? Who was the naughtiest person in the class?
- What actually is your job? What do you do all day? If you didn't have to work what would you do?
- What is the most dangerous thing you've ever done?
- What makes you scared?
- What is the naughtiest thing you've ever done?
- Have you ever lived in another country? Would you like to live there again?
- What was Mummy/Daddy like when they were my age? Which of my aunts and uncles was the naughtiest? Did you fight with your brother?
- Who is your best friend?
- What was it like when you got married? Did you ever get married before that?
- Have you ever been to hospital? Have you ever had stitches?
- Why do you get cross if I don't tidy my room? Did you tidy your room when you were little? Honestly?

And here are some for grown-ups to ask children:

- Who is your best friend and why? Have you ever had an argument with them?
- Would you rather live in the town or the country? What do you like about it?
- What kind of pet would you have if you could have anything at all? What would you call it?

- What's your favourite thing about school? And your least favourite?
- What makes you scared? Angry? Laugh?
- What's the most exciting holiday you've been on?
- Did you by any chance spot where I put the car keys?

SEVENS

You will need a ball for this game, and a wall or garage door to bounce it against. A football, a tennis ball or a beach ball are all fine. A cricket ball is not so good as it's too hard and doesn't bounce very well. You can play on your own, or take it in turns with any number of players.

SEVEN times, throw the ball against the wall and catch it.

SIX times, throw the ball against the wall, let it bounce on the ground once and then catch it.

FIVE times, bounce the ball on the floor with the palm of one hand (like a basketball player) and then catch it.

FOUR times, bounce the ball off the floor, then off the wall and then catch it (the opposite of Sixes).

THREE times, throw the ball against the wall, clap

your hands twice and then catch it.

TWO times, throw the ball under your leg, bounce it off the wall and then catch it.

ONE time, throw the ball against the wall, turn right around and then catch it.

There are plenty of ways to vary Sevens – touch the ground, do it with one hand, stand on one leg, stand further away from the wall each time. We used to play 'Stillses', which is where you have to keep your feet in exactly the same spot, except for lifting up one leg for Twoses, and turning around for Oneses. See what variations you can come up with.

STUCK IN THE MUD

Be prepared to get dirty hands and knees in this game. The more people you can get to join in, the better. Decide on boundaries for the game, so that no one wanders off and gets lost.

One person is 'it' and they must chase the others and try to touch them. If you are touched (even a tiny little touch!), then you must stand up straight with your arms above your head and your legs apart. You can be freed only by another person crawling underneath your legs and out the other side. The person who is freeing you is 'safe' and cannot be caught while actually crawling through.

We sometimes play a version that is called Melting Candles: when you are caught you stand in the same way, but you slowly sink to the ground, making it harder to be freed. If you end up collapsed and melted on the floor, then you become an 'it' as well, and now try to catch the others.

When everybody is stuck in the mud with no one left to free them, a new person can be 'it'. Or you'll be exhausted and stop anyway.

If there are lots of wheezy adults playing, then we suggest that you mark out a little patch with sticks or sweaters (or it could be a park bench) and call it 'home'. This is a safe place where you cannot be caught. However, only one person at a time is allowed in there. If someone else jumps in then you must jump out, even if you have only been there for two seconds. Sometimes it just isn't fair, but then that's the game!

BILLY GOAT SPLASH

This is a game of daring and bleating. Choose someone to be the troll, and the rest are goats.

Place sticks on the ground to form two parallel rows, about six feet long and two feet apart. If you can't find sticks, then use a couple of sweaters, coats or rows of stones instead. This is the bridge. At one end of the bridge place a pile of treasure – about fifteen different things which need to be collected. This could be shoes, or pennies, or conkers, or apples, or pebbles, or coloured leaves... whatever you have to hand. Probably not boulders.

The goats sit at the other end of the bridge to the treasure, bleating 'baa... baaa!' The troll sits close to the side of the bridge with his eyes closed and his back turned, so he cannot see the treasure, the goats or the bridge. Then one of the goats must try to creep over the bridge to collect a piece of treasure and get back to the herd without being heard. The other goats must carry on bleating to try to disguise any trit-trot sound of hooves.

Meanwhile, the troll must listen very carefully. When he thinks that he can hear a goat on the bridge he shouts 'SPLASH!' and turns around to see if he has caught anyone. If any part of a goat is on the bridge then they are kidnapped, and must go and sit by the troll. However, if there are no goats on the bridge then the troll must give up a piece of treasure. The game ends when all the treasure has been collected or all the goats are captured.

The goats can try to trick the troll into thinking that there is someone on the bridge by bleating extra loudly, or making running noises with their feet. And if the troll succeeds in catching all the goats he may of course sing 'I'm a troll, fol-de-rol' and proceed to eat the goats for his supper.

BUG RUMMAGING

In most woods, gardens or along country lanes, you can rummage for bugs by turning over a stone, flowerpot or pieces of bark and logs. In one single bug-hunting expedition recently we found centipedes, earwigs, spiders, ants' nests, an orange slug, millipedes, beetles, worms and woodlice galore. Anything that you don't know the name of is called an ibboo.

Have a pokey stick handy, and if, like Suzy, you are not too fond of creepy crawlies, then try to be brave. Soon you will discover that they're really not so much frightening as fascinating.

MAKING A DEN

As children we made some dens that were so ridiculously dangerous it's amazing we're here to tell the tale. There was a particularly precarious log house, supremely engineered by our cousin Sophie, with big, heavy planks on the top. Kelvin Wheatcroft kicked it down while we were inside it. We escaped with a few bruises, but unfortunately Kelvin was the victim of a mysterious attack later that summer at a village disco. Some angry girls put a blanket over his head, stole his trousers, and threw them into the pond. Poor Kelvin had to run all the way home in his pants, while the girls hid behind the bus shelter laughing!

Building a den is the very essence of childhood. A secret place, where adults are only permitted by invitation. It can be stuffed full with 'borrowed' items, like Granny's best quilt and a few cushions, a plastic yoghurt pot filled with stolen raspberries, and crisps and sweets of course. We even made fires and boiled eggs from the hen house for our tea. It was the very pinnacle of independence for nine-year-olds.

How you make a den depends entirely on the materials available. If you are in a small back garden, you can sling a blanket or sheet over the washing line and secure it on either side with stones or logs. If you are out in the park, you might find a branch hanging down low that you can turn into a hiding place with some coats. An umbrella makes an excellent roof. But if you have the great good fortune to be in the woods or fields then there will be a wealth of natural building materials: fallen branches, logs, sticks, leaves, bracken, grasses, stones, hay bales and much more. If you can purloin some bin liners to put on the ground, you won't get such a wet bottom when you sit down.

Please tell your children never to light fires without someone responsible with them, but do let them cook a sausage supper, or toast marshmallows on long sticks. It's a memory that will last for ever.

WHAT'S THE TIME, MR WOLF?

This is a huge success, particularly with little children, whose squealing and excited giggling must surely be one of the best sounds in the world.

Choose one person to be Mr Wolf, while the rest of you are sheep. Make a line on the floor and get all the sheep to stand behind it. Mr Wolf stands with his back to the sheep, about ten yards away.

All the sheep then call out 'WHAT'S THE TIME, MR WOLF?', and whatever o'clock he calls, the sheep must take that many steps towards him. So if he answers 'Seven o'clock!' they must each take seven steps, 'One o'clock!' means one step, and so on.

When the wolf judges that the sheep are pretty close behind him, and he is asked the time, he can shout out 'DINNERTIME!' He then whirls round and tries to catch the fleeing sheep, who must run back to the start without being caught. Any sheep that is captured becomes a wolf too. Continue until the last sheep is caught.

TOP TIP: Really young children like to hold someone's hand so that they don't get too frightened, and can be helped back over the line.

BOAT BUILDING

If you are lucky enough to be having a day out by a babbling brook, then here is a gorgeous way to while away an hour.

Make a little boat. The very best ones that we've ever made were fashioned out of good pieces of bark, but you can also try small bits of branch. With some types of soft wood you can poke a stick in to make a mast. A large leaf threaded onto a twig makes a fine sail. You can then race your vessels down the stream. Poking with long sticks is allowed if your boat gets stuck on a bank, or tangled up with some weeds, but pushing your boat downstream is cheating!

At a recent Barratt family party, cousin Dylan gallantly waded waist-deep to keep everyone's boats in the main channel, while the rest of us kept beautifully dry feet running through the meadow following the race.

We're sure you don't need to be reminded, but ALWAYS supervise children playing in or near water.

TODDLER'S DELIGHT

If you are going on a walk with a very young child — one who can walk pretty well but who has a tendency to want shoulder rides — here are a few tips on how to have a successful jaunt. Most of these diversions work with older children too.

Go slowly. Look ahead all the time for something to take their interest, and then get really interested in it yourself.

A few examples include:

- Thistledown to blow off their hand, like fairies
- Blackberries to pick and eat
- Snails to find under flowerpots
- Four-leafed clover to search for

- Trees to climb
- Beetles and slugs to inspect
- Dandelion clocks to blow
- Stiles to negotiate
- Huge leaves to use as fans
- Sticks to throw really far
- Low walls to walk along
- Steps to jump up and down
- Branches to bounce on
- Gates to open and close and climb over
- Puddles to jump in
- Horses to pat
- Cows to moo at
- Sheep to sing to

If you have a dog lead or a bit of string, tie it onto yourself and let them pull you along. Or tie it loosely round their middle and pull them up a hill. Let them win a race to the next corner. Sing 'The Grand Old Duke of York'.

The key is to be in the same frame of mind as them. It doesn't matter if it all takes a bit longer. If you let them know that you are in a hurry, they will almost certainly drag their heels more!

It's different, of course, if you have older children with you too, but if you have the luxury of an hour outside with a toddler, then go at their pace, give in to their ideas and rediscover the joys of carefree, idle busyness.

HUGGING TREES

This is the point at which accusations of old-hippiedom are likely to start flying, but hugging trees is a really pleasurable experience. Teenagers particularly should be encouraged to do this, as it has a curiously calming effect. Our mum was often muttering wishes up to the branches as she clung to a tree trunk with her eyes closed, and she definitely felt better for it. Give it a go. It'll make you smile.

Find a tree that you like the look of. Big oaks and beech trees are especially fine, but a small silver birch sapling has its own allure too. The texture of the bark will change from tree to tree, and so will the temperature, depending on whether the sun is shining on it or not. Now wrap your arms around, press your cheek against it, and have a little think and a wish. Look up at the branches above, and the leaves blowing in the breeze, and the puffy white clouds scudding across the sky. Breathe deeply and feel the benefit!

POOH STICKS

Made famous by A. A. Milne and the Winnie the Pooh books, this enduringly popular pastime is still a winner.

Location is pretty essential here. You need to be standing on a footbridge with a river or stream flowing beneath it. Size doesn't matter. We've played it on big lock bridges over the Thames and a tiny stream in North Wales with a stone slab over it.

Each choose a stick. Compare them so that you can distinguish between them from a distance, e.g. 'Mine's the long one with a twiggy bit at the end.' Stand on the upstream side of the bridge, then, after a count of three, all drop them into the water. (You're not allowed to cheat and aim them under the bridge like our cousin Pippa always did!) Then run to the other side of the bridge and see which stick comes out first. There seems to be no advantage to having a big or small stick, or which bank you stand closest to. Keep going with new sticks until everyone has won at least once. You can also use leaves and bark. Try not to fall in, and hold the hands of small children very tightly.

SKIPPITY SKIP

We used to get such bad giggles playing this. A pretty silly game, but one that we still enjoy.

One of you gets up and skips from A to B and back again to A, while saying out loud, 'Skippity skip, skippity skip.' Everyone else must watch, noting carefully every single move and noise you make. Notice how the person skipping holds their arms or how long it takes them to turn around. Maybe they nearly lose their balance at one point or have to stop and cough. Clock their facial expression – what are their eyes and mouth doing? There is only one rule: when you are skipping, you must concentrate and do your finest skipping.

The skipper then sits back down again and nominates someone else to copy them. The chosen person must do their very best imitation of the last skipper, trying to remember everything that they did, and exaggerating, of course. It is then the imitator's turn to skip properly and another's chance to mimic.

HARES AND HOUNDS

This event needs lots of you and a little bit of preparation. But it is fantastically good fun, and leaves everyone exhausted and ready for a huge lunch. The Barratt clan is exceptionally good at this game.

A large number of people is what is needed; anything over four will work, but if gets really exciting when there are nine or ten of you. Two people who know the area are chosen as the hares. Then they set off, running if they can, but certainly going at a brisk pace. They take with them a bag of flour, or hay, or sawdust, or finely shredded newspaper, which will decompose over time, and lay a trail as they go, putting a little pile of whatever they have about every thirty yards. If they want they can leave arrows made from sticks on the ground.

After about fifteen minutes everyone else can set off. They are the hounds, so if the hounds at the front of the pack find a pile of flour they bark, howl or bay to let the stragglers know which direction to follow, and also to let the hares know how close they are getting. If the hares want to, they can lay a few false trails, doubling back on themselves and going off in a new direction. It's also worth putting a few Crunchie bars in an obvious place (e.g. on top of a stile, at the foot of a tree or next to a pile of sawdust). The chocolate serves both as an incentive for the hounds, and as a tactic to slow them down while they share them out. Sometimes the hounds will catch up with the hares; sometimes the hares will make it to the pub, or back to the car, or home, first. If you only give them a five-minute head start it's pretty even. The point is not winning or losing, but eating chocolate, running till you are really out of breath, and having extra roast potatoes and gravy at the end of it all.

BONKERS FOR CONKERS

OK, so you have all had fun collecting conkers. But what do you do with the shining brown beauties stuffed into every pocket?

Instead of skewering the conkers (and yourself) on bits of string to make vicious knuckle-rappers, keep them in your pockets for the rest of the afternoon and carry on your walk until you find a suitable place to rest a while. Then look around to see if there is a puddle, a thick branch or the trunk of a tree, a small patch of mud, anything that you can use for target practice, and toss your conkers at your target, scoring out loud as you go. You can either all fire at the same target or have individual ones, but make sure no one is too near the target — conkers really hurt if they get you in the wrong place.

Polly's son, Jojo (being a typical boy and mad about anything that he is allowed to throw), once spent an entire afternoon trying to throw conkers into a bucket after he had got home from the park. When he ran out of conkers in his pocket he simply went up to the bucket, tipped it upside down, refilled his pockets, uprighted the bucket and started all over again, and again, and again...

GRANDMOTHER'S FOOTSTEPS

This is such a classic and a winner for younger children.

One of you is Granny (preferably Granny if she is around, or maybe a grown-up for the first game while everyone gets used to it). Granny stands twenty feet or so away from all the others with her back turned. While she is not looking, everyone must silently creep towards her. Whenever she turns round, all of you must stop moving immediately. If Granny sees any feet moving at all, she can order their owners back to the initial starting point and they will have to try creeping up all over again. There are no rules as to how many times she can turn round, but she should allow enough time in between turns for everyone to take a couple of steps. Whoever manages to reach Granny first and tickle her, gets to be Granny in the next round. Remember: it is only feet that must not be seen moving — the odd sway or correction of balance is allowed.

We played an excellent version of this game after a

magical picnic in the middle of
some bluebell woods in Dorset. All
the grown-ups were feeling a little sleepy
and so were allowed to lie down on the rugs
with their eyes shut. All the children
gathered at a tree about thirty feet
away and had to creep up on us,
without us being able to hear them. If
we heard any whispering or any twigs
breaking under their feet, they all
had to start again. They loved it and
we got a few minutes' kip in the
sunshine – perfect.

52 BUNKEROO

This game conjures up so many happy memories. We were incredibly fortunate to grow up having access to a huge communal garden. We spent every summer evening in huge gangs, chasing each other through long grass and stealing secret kisses from our childhood sweethearts. Even the inevitable hay fever and awkward heartbreak couldn't quench our thirst for this game — plenty of running, plenty of shouting, and plenty of opportunities to hide secretly with other people.

First of all, choose your 'base'. This needs to be an obvious place that you can run to — a big old tree, a park bench, a pile of jumpers on the floor, anything you can call base. One of you is 'It', stays at base with their eyes shut and counts fairly swiftly to fifty-two.

Everyone else has to run away and hide. Choose your hiding place well. You want to be able to peek out now and again and see what It is up to and where they are in relation to the chosen base.

When It has finished counting, they must have a good look and wander around a bit to see if they can see anyone hiding. If they do spot someone, they must run back to base and shout '52 Bunkeroo, I see Ella over by the long grass.' Ella must then walk back to base and wait. If, however, Ella has already realised that she has been spotted, she can try and race It back to base. If she touches base first, she can shout '52 Bunkeroo, I'm in' and is safe. At any stage of the game, anyone who is hiding can hedge their bets and try to run for base if they think they can get back before It spots them running and makes for base as well.

Inevitably, people do get caught in this game – it's easier being It than being one of those who hides. The first person to be caught is usually It in the next round of the game. However, there is a chance that you can be rescued. Here's how. Once all of you bar one are back at base, you can shout 'SAVE ALL' to the last hider. They will then know it is crucial that they get back to base, proudly shouting '52 Bunkeroo, I save all,' before It does, thereby rescuing everyone. It's easy to see why gangly adolescents suddenly turned into heroes on those long, hot summer evenings.

LET'S GET DIZZY

This is real belly-laughing stuff. Nearly all kids love being made dizzy either by aeroplane acrobatics or roundabout action. But here are a few more ways to make yourself and your kids dizzy which might be kinder to your back and their shoulder sockets.

Put your finger on the end of your nose and direct your eyes to it so that you are practically cross-eyed. Keep your eye on the end of your nose and ask someone to help turn you around five times (adult brains may need ten spins to reach maximum dizziness). As soon as you have completed your five turns, take your finger off your nose and run to a designated person ten feet or so away. Make sure you are on soft ground − one of you is bound to fall over in collapsed hysterics.

If you can't quite get the end-of-the-nose idea, then simply put your arms out to the side and bend over so that your chin is practically in line with your knees. Keep looking at your feet as someone helps to propel you round as quickly as possible.

Other good things to try after five or ten turns: jumping, hopping (impossible), balancing on one leg, a somersault or just lying on the ground staring up at the sky (hey, man).

HUNT THE SHOE

This will absorb smaller children when you are in a fairly overgrown area or on a nice patch of grass surrounded by bushes. If you haven't got enough energy or inspiration for a full-blown treasure hunt then take the fabulously lazy option. Kick off your shoes, pick one of them up and find a crafty place to hide it — in the long grass, up a tree, sticking out of a bush, wherever.

Make sure everyone who wishes to join the hunt has their eyes closed and backs turned so that they will not be able to see where the shoe is hidden. Then sit and observe while everyone goes off to search for the shoe, giving clues and signs of encouragement if needed.

FOLLOW MY LEADER

An excellent way to get children to walk up that hill or go just that little bit further. Try this before you resort to piggybacks or chocolate bribes.

Form a line, one standing behind the other. The first person in the line is the leader and starts walking. After about five paces, the next person starts walking, then the next after another five paces and so on. If the leader decides to start marching, or striding slowly, or walking with their hands out to the side, then the next person in line should do the same, followed by the next person, etc.

Other good things to try as the leader include:

- Hopping
- Wiggling your bum around
- Clapping
- Singing a TV theme tune or advert
- Jumping
- Smelling a particular flower
- Walking as if your legs are giving up
- Blowing raspberries
- Leaping over a stile

It doesn't matter what you decide to do as the leader, but try to fit in something different to do every twenty paces or so.

When one person has had a good enough go at being the leader, send them to the back of the line and start again with a new leader.

DAISY CHAINS

A good quiet pastime that needs just three things — daisies (obviously), patience (sometimes hard to come by) and a good-length fingernail. We suspect that girls like making these more than boys do.

Pick two daisies, each with as long a stem as possible. Make a cut with your fingernail about halfway up one of the stems so that it looks a bit like an eye of a needle, i.e. there is still some stem surrounding the cut on all sides. Then thread the other daisy through the cut, being very careful that you do not rip the stem. Then make a cut in the stem of the daisy you have just threaded through and find another long-stemmed daisy to go through that cut. Keep going and make a bracelet, necklace, tiara or garland.

Very often it's not the daisy chains themselves that are the pleasure of this game. It's the conversations you have with your children while you are all busy with your hands, nobody necessarily looking at each other, just peacefully sitting down and helping each other out. Younger kids are fantastic at finding the daisies and concentrating on long stems, while older kids with more agile fingers love creating the finished line of jewellery.

GARDEN OBSTACLE COURSE

Obstacle courses are best done individually, with each racer competing in turn against the clock, seeing who can achieve the best time. Set these courses in the park or woods, and especially in the garden. Here are a few things that you could put into your course:

- Crawl under a garden chair
- Run backwards carrying a bucket of water
- Do a somersault, cartwheel or walk on your hands
- Jump over a watering can
- Walk along a wall, or balance on some upturned flowerpots
- Run around a tree
- Jump up or down steps
- Run in a pair of wellies much too big for you
- Crawl through a pile of leaves
- Put on a hat, scarf and gloves
- Do a three-point turn on a tricycle

Make certain that the course is properly set up each time, and be sure to have a go yourself. Your kids will like to see you falling over and looking silly!

WHACKY RACES

When you have had enough of normal running races, tried hopping, jumping and racing backwards, have a go at some of these.

Crab race: Get into pairs and face your partner. Both bend down, bottoms upwards, and grab hold of each other's ankles. Then race the other couples to a finishing line going sideways, without letting go. So while one of you is moving to the left, the other is going right.

Push-me-pull-you race: Stand back-to-back with a partner and link arms, then race other pairs up to a point and back again. On the way back, whichever one of you was going forwards now has to go backwards, and vice versa.

Spider race: Choose a partner. Crouch on all fours, then have your partner crouch on all fours over the top of you, but going across your back with their body, so that it looks a little like you have eight limbs. Then scuttle together around a circular course trying to gently knock into other spiders and distract and divert them.

Wheelbarrow race: Get into pairs. One person puts their hands on the ground, and the other one stands behind and picks up their legs. Together you race to the finishing line, trying not to fall over and bump your nose in the mud.

Pebble knees: This is a race in which you place a pebble about the size of a satsuma between your knees and then run. If your pebble falls to the ground you must start again.

Tortoise race: One person must be the judge and stand aside whilst everyone else is blindfolded and gets down on all fours at the starting line. When the judge says so, all tortoises should start to crawl as slowly as possible towards the finishing line. However, you must keep moving at all times. The judge is allowed to tell you at any time that you are remaining too motionless and, if deemed necessary, ban you from the course and turn you into a charming, but rather useless, antique cigarette box.

The aim of the race is to be neither the first nor the last to cross the finishing line (hence the need for blindfolds, so you can't see where everyone else is in relation to you). Thankfully, this means that you can have plenty of winners.

After the race, the tortoises can decide whether the judge was good and fair or too bossy, and are officially allowed to push the judge onto the ground and tickle until he or she apologises.

TREASURE HUNTS

We've included treasure hunts in other sections of this book because they are such fantastic things to do. The basic rule is that each person or team is given a variety of things to find. You can write lists and hand them out if you wish, or just call out a new object to look for each time something is found.

Here are some examples of things to choose from if you are out and about, in the park, garden, woods, fields or mountains:

A red leaf, an acorn, a fir cone, a fruit, a feather, a curved stick, a stick with a forked end, a wood louse, a rabbit dropping, a bit of wool, a bit of eggshell (no stealing from nests!), some moss, something blue, something beginning with M, a dandelion clock, a flying insect, a piece of straw, something that will hold water, something that someone has dropped, four blades of grass that are equal lengths, a daisy, a buttercup, an icicle, a singing member of the Von Trapp family...

HIGH JUMP

A little cheating is needed when playing this with young children, but those with long legs and good co-ordination should be able to manage it.

Find a stick about six feet long. Two people must then hold it a few inches off the ground, balancing it lightly on their fingers so that if it is knocked it will fall off. Each jumper then takes a run-up and tries to leap over the stick without knocking it off. Raise the stick a little higher each time, and see who can jump the highest. The cheating part is that, as very small children approach and take off, the stick-holders lower it almost to the ground and lift it back again once the child is over. Make sure the stick-holders get a chance to jump too, if they want to; some people, like Suzy, hate high jump.

When you have had enough of high jump, do a limbo dance instead. Start with the stick high, and go under it belly-up. Lower the stick each time, and see who can get under the lowest. You are supposed to go under with your chest facing upwards all the time, but the under-sixes that we know don't seem to be able to get the hang of it, so let them do it however they want!

UNDER-EIGHTEEN-MONTHS TODDLE OR CRAWLING RACE

This is exactly what it sounds like. We've included it because we wanted to remind everyone that really small people respond to races as well as larger ones, and that there are plenty of ways to ensure that they stand a good chance of winning. Either everyone has to copy the toddler's style of walking or everyone has to crawl, depending on which stage of development the youngster has reached. Crawling backwards often feels surprisingly strange and difficult, particularly with a hangover. Anyone who feels like a more experienced walker can always try to remember how to walk on his or her hands instead.

BIRDS' NESTS

If you can find the right kind of bendy sticks, young children adore making birds' nests.

Weave, bend and mould sticks into a small circle, and take it from there, adding grasses, moss, twigs, horse hair, wool and leaves. At Easter we like to make a nest to hide chocolate eggs in.

GRANDPA'S SIXPENCE

You can play this game if you are a grandpa, granny, aunt, uncle, godparent or just looking after a friend's kids for them. It does need a moment of preparation, but the delight on a small child's face is worth the effort.

If you have the grandchildren coming to stay with you, decide in advance where you might take them for a little walk. This could be to the shops, or woods, or park, or just down the garden. Then, some time beforehand, hide a small coin in a secret place: maybe under a stone, or brick, or in a tree trunk. As you approach it with your young brood, weave a story about how fairies live near here and sometimes leave money under this special stone. Elaborate as you see fit. Then let them look in the hiding place and find the treasure.

If you are fortunate to have the same children staying regularly, they will soon make visiting the fairy stone an essential part of their exciting stay. Even if they have an inkling that fairies don't really exist, they will love joining in with the possibility that maybe, just maybe...

I'M BORED! ...

ON A BEACH

SEAWEED WIGS

Collect up seaweed from along the beach, then drape it on your head for a splendid new look. Try different kinds to see which suits you the best, and remember to shake the seaweed well to dislodge any lurking crabs or unwelcome creepy-crawlies.

For the very brave, you could try some particularly slimy green seaweed (sometimes called sea lettuce) as a rather fetching beard or moustache and eyebrows. Why not ask someone to judge you, and award a bottle of sweet-smelling shampoo as the prize?

FLOTSAM COLLAGES

These are very popular with both children and adults. The only time that it is hard to do them is when the wind is blowing up a real hooley.

Take a wander down the beach and collect up anything that catches your eye: bits of fabric, plastic, rope and string, driftwood and twigs, polystyrene, interesting pebbles, seaweed, palm leaves, coconuts, shoes... anything interesting and colourful that is lying around.

We find that it's best to gather together all your flotsam and then see if an idea leaps out at you. Once we found an old pair of swimming goggles, which we thought could be a pair of glasses, and that gave us the idea to make a girl going to school. She had a very fine multi-coloured school uniform, made from different scraps of coloured material, and bunches in her seaweed and rope hair, and a splendid satchel formed from half a flipper and a salty belt. Her lips were made from bottle tops, her nose from half a tennis ball, and we used pebbles as an outline for good definition. Generally, figures and faces work well, and don't forget to add jewellery, shoes, hats, bags and maybe a parrot on a pirate's shoulder.

If there is nothing on the beach except seaweed and pebbles, they too can make a lovely collage. Use pebbles that are the same colour to create blocks and shapes, and white stones as outlines. You could try a picture of a boat, using pebbles for the boat and seaweed as a churning sea around it.

Other ideas are fishes, sea monsters, mermaids, houses, flowers and animals.

A finished collage or any piece of beach art will look even better if you make a frame for it. Use pebbles, seaweed, driftwood, or just build a low wall of sand around it. A framed masterpiece is also much more noticeable to passers-by. In North Carolina, where people drive onto the beach in their jeep-loads, a simple picture with an obvious frame was left untouched for days. You could see from the tyre marks that everyone had swerved to avoid it.

MOUSE DINNER PARTIES

Little kids especially love this, and it really gets them using their imaginations.

Lay out a towel or T-shirt as a picnic rug and find some small flat stones as mouse-sized dinner plates. Then look around and see what you could find that might look like food. Here are some pointers to get you started:

- Little shells with a twig sticking out of them might be chicken drumsticks.
- A bit of seaweed could be cabbage or broccoli.
- Can you find some tiny pebbles for roast potatoes?
- Would the mice like tiny boiled eggs in tiny egg cups?
- Can you find something that would do as little cups and saucers?
- What could they have for pudding?
- Do they need knives and forks, or napkins?

You can go on and on inventing all sorts of food depending on what you find on the beach. And, of course, your mouse guests will eat up everything, leaving their plates squeaky clean!

THREE-LEGGED RACE

A classic race which you can make a bit more tricky by using seaweed to tie your ankle to your partner's ankle. If the seaweed breaks you must stop and re-tie it.

Another variation on this game is a five-legged race, with three people tying their ankles together.

TOP TIP: Let the person in the middle decide which leg goes first, and have a packet of crisps ready to soothe any tears from tumbles.

SMALLEST SHELL COMPETITION

Exactly what it sounds like: who can find the smallest shell? This is a hunt for everyone, which can take as long as you like. There is only one rule: the shell must be intact, with no chips or holes.

Also in this category is the heart-shaped stone competition, or the most circular stone, or a stone with a hole in it.

When we play this, the winner gets an extra chocolate Flake in their teatime ice cream.

TREASURE HUNTS

Everyone loves these. Treasure hunts can be played in teams or individually, but it's great when the older ones help the little ones a bit. You might need to organise yourself a bit beforehand by writing down lists to hand out, or you can just make it up as you go along, calling out the next object to hunt for as an item is found.

The basic idea is to give each team a number of things to find, and the first one back with all of them, or the team who has found the most items in an agreed time limit, is the winner.

The kind of beach you are on will tend to determine what is reasonable to find, but here's a list that you could choose from: a piece of string, a crab's claw, a bit of red plastic, a feather, three perfectly white pebbles, two perfectly round stones, something with writing on, something that holds water, a piece of fishing line, something that used to be alive, a stick with a v-shaped top, a stone with a hole right through it, something beginning with B, something shiny, something that nobody else has found, something smelly, something yellow, a scrap of blue material, an abandoned shoe, a coconut, something that is still alive (this can include a lost child or granny), something that fell off a boat, just ten grains of sand (much more difficult than it sounds!), a mermaid's purse, a limpet shell, something that floats, something that sinks, a lolly wrapper, an albatross covered in an oil slick... Try to include a mix of the easy and the adventurous!

THE PEBBLE AND DRIFTWOOD RACE

A beach version of an egg and spoon race, using a suitable piece of driftwood or plastic to balance a pebble on. Remember, if you drop your pebble you must go back to the start.

If you want to make this game even more challenging, an impartial onlooker can throw buckets of water at anyone they believe may have an unfair advantage (or who has annoyed them in some trivial way). CAUTION: This added hindrance should only be included on a warmish day, and with a sense of humour.

TOP TIP: The key to winning this is to choose your carrying object carefully and to take it slowly.

UNCLE RALPH'S COMFY CHAIR

You know how hard it can be to get really comfortable on the beach sometimes? If you lie flat on your back, your arms get tired holding your trashy novel and the sun in your eyes makes you squint. If you lie on your front, you get a crick in your neck and sand on your chin and your book is too close to your eyes. Here at last is the solution.

This was first shown to us by a friend in Australia, and it has revolutionised relaxing on the beach for us, particularly when heavily pregnant and extremely ungainly. It's called Uncle Ralph's Comfy Chair because Uncle Ralph loves to relax and hates the word comfy.

Here's what you do. In the place where you would like to sit, face the sea then stand with your legs apart, bend over and dig like a dog with your front paws. Pile up all the sand that comes out of the hole to make a mound behind the hole. Depending on the size of your bottom, the hole should be about eighteen inches deep and wide, and the mound about two feet high. When you have patted it all down firmly and maybe put a sprinkling of warm, dry sand or your towel in the hole, settle down. Your bottom goes in the hole, your back and head rest against the gently sloping mound, and your legs are slightly bent and raised in front of you. Bliss, we promise.

SHADOW DRAWINGS

Try this on a sandy beach, at the end of the day when shadows are getting longer and tempers are getting shorter.

It needs two of you, one to be the model and the other to be the artist. The model strikes a pose that makes an interesting silhouette – maybe arms out to the side, one leg in the air or fingers coming out like antlers on top of your head – then has to stay totally still. The artist then sets to work and quickly traces the outline of the silhouette in the sand.

How about trying to make yourself into each of the letters that spell out your name? (But be prepared for awkward positions, losing your balance and looking as if you are dancing to 'YMCA'.)

BOAT RACES

If you are lucky enough to be on a beach with a stream running through it, you can have a peaceful and serene regatta or fiercely competitive boat races.

Boats can be made from all sorts of things: bits of polystyrene, cork or wood will all bob along nicely. You can decorate them with a twig mast and a paper sail, or a driftwood rudder or a pebble engine. As they float downstream they may encounter obstacles on the way which you can remove, or dig deeper channels if need be. You can also throw stones at them and try to get them to sink.

Experiment with larger boats made from a piece of driftwood, balance pebbles and shells and seaweed on them as their cargo, and see how far they get before you have a major shipping disaster.

Our tremendous Aunt Ros has decided that when she dies she wants her ashes placed on a driftwood boat and sent down a stream and off into the Atlantic on a moonlit night!

STONE TOWERS

A quiet game for those who aren't in the mood for running around. Find some flat, or flattish, stones and pebbles. Start with the larger ones at the bottom and see how high you can make a tower. Balancing as you go along is the key, and you may find that a stone that made the tower wobble too much when further down, is just perfect two stones higher. If you can balance nine, that's pretty impressive.

A series of stone towers in a line along the beach looks fantastic, and if you build them where the tide will come in over them, you can try to guess which one will stay up the longest. The more destructive members of your group can also enjoy throwing stones at them to try to knock them down.

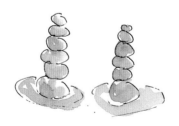

LIMPET NOSE

Limpets are the conical shellfish that live on rocks and are impossible to prise off. However, look along the shore and you will almost certainly find empty shells. If there are no limpets, experiment with other shells.

Find one limpet shell per person. Draw a starting and finishing line in the sand. Balance the limpet shell on your nose by tipping your head back, and then run like crazy. If your limpet falls off your nose (which it probably will), go back to the start. Watch out for stubbed toes in this one – it's hard to look down with your head tipped back.

To play Limpet Eyes, choose two limpet shells each and put them over your eyes instead. There'll be even more stubbed toes with this game, and you might bump into each other as well.

Why not go the whole hog? Put shells on your nose and eyes, and then another balanced on pouting lips.

TOP TIP: Check for hermit crabs before attempting these races!

LONG JUMP

This event is for sandy beaches only; it can be hard on the toes otherwise.

Draw a take-off line and have as long a run-up as you like. Draw a line out to the side to mark where you landed, so that you can judge yourself against the others. For variation try jumping without a run-up, or try jumping backwards.

Be sure to cheer each other along during the run-ups. The winner gets a sandy apple.

DAM IT ALL!

If on your beach you have even a trickle of water, then you need look no further for something for the grown-up men to do. It is a proven sociological fact that fathers find it impossible to sit back and watch a dam being constructed without joining in and bagsying the best spade, ordering everyone else on the beach to keep an eye on one bit of the barrier or other, and sending small children off in search of enormous rocks, which they will dutifully heave back to him before carefully dropping them on their own toes.

Dams are fantastic. Whether you have only sand to pile high to try and hold back the flow to form a lake, or whether you are on a stony beach and become an expert in drystone-walling in order to accomplish a diversion of the water, dams can use up a whole day.

If where you are building your fortification there is a bit of a pong, be aware that you might be damming a sewage outlet. There was often a worried cry from Granny, 'What about the sewage?' whenever we started on our waterworks, but as far as we can remember, we never caught cholera or dysentery.

See if you can divert the stream so that it takes a completely new path, using walls and ditches, or form a big lake by blocking the stream completely. You will need to keep working on this, as the fuller the lake gets, the higher and wider you will have to dam.

HOPSCOTCH

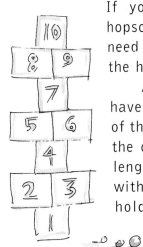

If you have forgotten how to play hopscotch, here's our version. You will need to be on a sandy beach to draw the hopscotch pitch.

A quick recap of the rules: you have to throw your pebble on to each of the numbered squares, starting with the closest, and then hop or jump the length of the pitch and back again without landing on the square that holds your pebble. For example, throw the stone on to square number one, then jump over square one landing on squares two and three, then hop on to four, jump on to five and six, hop on to seven, jump on to eight and nine, then hop on to ten. Then, balancing carefully, turn round on one leg and hopscotch back again, stopping at number two to pick up your pebble, and jump back over number one.

Then throw your pebble on to square two, hop on to square one, hop on to three, hop on to four, jump on to five and six, etc., all the way to ten and back again, stopping at square number three to pick up your stone.

FLIPSTONES, MEET THE FLIPSTONES

Sit down with ten tiny rounded pebbles in front of you. Pick up a stone and place it in the palm of one hand. Throw it up into the air and flip your hand over so that you catch it with the back of your hand. Throw it up again, flipping your hand back once more, catching it in your palm this time. If you have managed to do this without dropping the pebble you can shout 'YABBA-DABBA-DOO'. Now pick up another pebble and try doing the same flips with two stones, then three, then four and so on. You reach official genius status if you can do this with all ten pebbles.

TOP TIP: Keep your fingers firmly together to stop the stones from falling through.

BLINDFOLD RACE

This is one of our favourite races, not least because of the looks you get from other people on the beach – a mixture of admiration, envy and confusion.

Get into pairs – little ones with big ones is obviously the fairest combination. One of you is the runner and the other is the guide. The runner is blindfolded with a T-shirt, sweater or towel, whatever you have to hand, and stands on the starting line.

You can now make the game as difficult as you like. In the simplest version, the guides must stand behind the starting line and shout directions to their runner, instructing them up to a chosen point (maybe a rock, a pile of seaweed or a bucket), round the obstacle and back to where they started. Sounds pretty easy, huh? Just remember there will be other people shouting directions to their runners at the same time, which gets extremely confusing.

Make the race even harder by drawing a course in the sand, and digging holes that must be jumped over.

TOP TIP: Shout encouraging things as well as instructions!

JACKS

This is an excellent game if your energy levels are flagging, and you need some one-handed catching practice.

Take six stones. One stone is for throwing up in the air, and we call this the Jill. Lay out the remaining five stones in front of you. These are your Jacks. Throw the Jill in the air, and with the same hand pick up one of the Jacks before catching the Jill. Then transfer the first jack into your other hand and repeat the process with the other four Jacks.

When you have been successful at picking up the jacks individually, move on to picking them up two by two, then three and two, then four and one, finally picking up all five at the same time before catching the Jill with the same hand.

Apparently, with practice you can get really good at this. Granny Lily is fiendishly good (although she does cheat occasionally). Suzy, on the other hand, is hopeless. Her school reports consistently pointed out how useless she was at throwing and catching, and she hasn't improved in twenty-five years.

SWIMMING ON DRY LAND

If you are on a completely pebbly beach that is very hard to run along, then this is a tremendous race which children find much easier than adults. It leaves you breathless and chortling.

Everyone lies on their stomachs on the pebbles, as if on a starting line. Decide between you where the finishing line is, and at a shout of 'GO!' everyone must propel themselves forward as though they are swimming. It's ridiculously hard work, and the sheer effort of it merits a large chunk of Kit-Kat to the winner.

STONE BOULES

Boys particularly love this game. It becomes quite addictive, and can be played in a wandering fashion, all along the beach and back.

First collect your stones. You need to find one smallish round stone that is easy to spot. Each player then needs to find three larger stones that they can distinguish as their own, either by their markings or by scratching a letter on them with a chalky pebble.

One of the players must throw the small stone, as near or as far as they like, and then everyone takes it in turns to throw one of their own stones, aiming to get it as close to the small stone as possible. Whoever lands one of their stone boules closest to the small stone gets to throw the small stone at the beginning of the next game.

While you all decide who is the winner, it is important to stand around making French noises with your hands on your hips.

PRIZE-WINNING SANDCASTLES

Building sandcastles is still one of the most fun things to do in the world. From a simple mound of sand with one carefully chosen shell on top to an elaborate maze of tunnels, towers and moats, sandcastles are simply one of the finest ways to while away an afternoon.

Here are a few ideas and tips for top creations. Mix and match as you like.

- Dig a trench – square or round or oval, whatever you fancy – but leave a portion of it undug so that you can tunnel underneath it and make a little bridge entrance to your castle. Pile all the sand that you have dug out into the middle to make a good-sized mound which you can then decorate with seaweed, stones, shells, sticks and flotsam.
- When you have forgotten the bucket and spade, or when the sand is too coarse and pebbly to turn into immaculate sandcastles, then make a wonderful Shell Mountain. Simply scoop up a mound with your forearms, the bigger the better, and pat it down firmly. Then decorate every available inch of space with shells or pebbles. The result is surprisingly beautiful. This works really well for smaller children as it does not need any special artistic know-how nor is it at all fiddly.
- Use the edge of a spade to cut in a long flight of

steps up the front of your sandcastle. This instantly adds a palatial feel.

- Make a flag to go on the top from a stick and some seaweed, and find some more greenery to make a garden on the slopes of the mound.
- After making a smooth mound of sand, carve a helter-skelter around the sides, working from top to bottom.

TOP TIP: Watch out for dogs. For some reason, sandcastles are their favourite things to do a wee on, although our dog was always very obliging and only went on other people's sandcastles.

OBSTACLE COURSE

Although you can all do this at the same time, we think there is more fun to be had if an obstacle course is done one by one, with someone timing for the winner. This way, you get to watch everyone else making a fool of themselves too.

A good obstacle course will include as many of the following as you feel like setting up: a trench to jump over (maybe filled with water); a shell to balance on your head or nose; a line to walk along that you mustn't fall off; a pair of shoes to wear that are too big (or too small); a towel to crawl under; a bucket of water to tip over your own head (warm weather only!); a mound to climb over; a line of four stones to balance on top of each other; Granny's hat to put on; specific areas where you must walk like a crab, do a cartwheel, run backwards, do two somersaults, build a sandcastle with your feet, etc.

Be sure to put the course back together again before the next contestant steps up.

EXHIBITION STONES

This is good on any beach with a few stones, shells and a tide line. It's a gentle, contemplative pastime for any age that can use up an hour of cloudy skies.

Find a decent-sized, flat stone not too far from where you have made camp, and brush off any sand and debris. Then hunt around on the beach for anything worthy to display on it: coloured glass with the edges all rounded off (usually known as jewels), perfect shells, a crab's claw, a mermaid's purse, a coconut shell, a bottle top, a feather; anything that you consider good enough to go into the exhibition.

Then arrange your treasure on the chosen exhibition stone and invite people to come and look while you explain what everything is. If it's really good you can charge 5p a visit!

SHIPWRECKED

Choose a good spot in the sand where the tide will come in later on.

Draw the shape of a boat, as if looking at it from above, with its bow pointing towards the sea. Hollow out the sand inside the boat and pile it up to make the sides of the vessel. Then dig a moat around the outside of the boat, again using the displaced sand to pile the sides up even higher.

Once you have the basic structure you can start to add the finer details should you so wish. Build up a seat inside with sand, or use some driftwood and make a steering wheel with a flat stone or bucket. If you can find a couple of long sticks and a beach towel you could make a sail too. More driftwood could make some oars or a rudder.

Then play in your boat and wait for the racing tide to come in and surround you. We like to keep the sides of the boat diligently piled up, getting increasingly hysterical and frantic as the water encroaches, trying to patch holes as they appear, until inevitably our sound ship is water-logged and ship-wrecked.

Other kinds of transport are good too. Try a car (with front and back seats), or even an aeroplane (with rows and rows of seats).

SAND SCULPTURES

These are an alternative to sandcastles for those feeling a little more adventurous. Mould wet sand into shapes and figures to make 3-D pictures. Try making a reclining figure; mermaids work particularly well because you don't have to worry about fiddly below-the-waist bits, and long fish-tails are nice and smooth. You may, however, need to do bosoms, which can be a moment of great merriment. (It's worth betting an ice cream that Dad will think he knows best!)

Once you know how to do mermaid tails, turn anyone who fancies a quick sit-down into a mermaid. Ask them to stretch their legs out in front of them, then cover their legs with sand and add the v-shaped tail just below their feet. If they are still enjoying a sit-down, then start marking out scales on the mermaid's tail.

Other ideas are sea monsters (a good choice if your reclining figure has gone wrong – just add a few more legs and an extra eye or two!), fishes, faces, animals, or a sphinx (that is really

DRIPPY CASTLES

This is a lovely solitary activity, and a good one to cool off a bit. Hot toes can be dabbled in the shallows at the same time.

Sit where the sand is pretty wet and scoop up a handful of sand. Let the sand drip off the ends of your fingers to make a little drippy pile so that it looks a bit like dripping candle wax. When the sand stops dripping easily off your fingertips, discard what is left in your hand, take up another scoop of wet sand and repeat. Soon you will learn the optimum amount of sand and water to form the best drip. Then you can build up any shape of magical castle you choose.

Our sister Emma did this for hours on a Greek beach when she was fourteen and head-over-heels in love with someone whose name she couldn't pronounce. She hoped he would notice her as she sat looking beautiful and dreamy.

FIFTEEN-TO-ONE

This is a game for two players that is best for older children, and people who like to figure puzzles out.

Choose fifteen stones – any size, any shape. Lay them out on the ground in three rows, five stones in each. Taking it in turns, each person takes away one, two, three, four or even five stones, but all must come from the same row.

The person who is forced to pick up the very last stone is the loser, but they get to start the next game.

It sounds a very simple game, but it has you thinking tactically, and the last stages are fiendishly hard to fathom!

SLEEPING SHARKS

Be prepared for high-pitched screams and over-excited youngsters with this one.

This game doesn't have to involve an adult if you really don't fancy getting wet, but the person who is the sleeping shark should be old enough to be able to float around in the shallows without swallowing too much sea water. If you do fancy trying to be the sleeping shark for a few goes, children always seem to get an extra thrill. Maybe they love the idea of lots of kids versus one adult, or maybe it's because, no matter how bad your shark impressions are, you can growl very loudly and scare them pretty easily.

So, decide who is going to be the shark. That

person lies down near the shoreline and lets themselves be rolled around by the lapping waves pretending to be asleep. All the other players must approach the shark one at a time, asking, 'Are you awake yet, Mr Shark?' Then with great caution they must try and prod the shark with their finger to see if the shark is indeed awake. The shark is allowed to ignore as many prods as he likes, until he feels it is truly time to wake up. Obviously the prodding has made the shark a little irritable, so he has every right to want to attack the prodders the moment he wakes, in which case he can just pounce and shout and try to catch someone, making as much noise and splash as possible.

Alternatively, he might want to wake up a little more slowly, and prolong the agony of everybody wondering who will be caught. If you are stuck for ideas about what to say, try something along the following lines to get you started. 'Who was it that just woke me up?' 'I've woken up starving hungry, so I'm going to find a nice little fish/girl/boy/aunty to eat.' 'Mmmm! I can smell somebody really close to me. Let me just check my teeth are sharp enough.' Then go for the attack.

AHOY THERE

A good game if you're getting a bit cold and damp and need to have a quick runaround.

Someone is picked as the shark, and everyone else is a sailor. The shark chases all the sailors, and if you are caught you must stand on one leg and call to the other sailors, 'Ahoy there, me hearties, I'm marooned!' or just 'Ahoy there, Ahoy there!' in a rather poor West Country accent. Hopefully someone will come to the rescue. The rescuer must draw a circle in the sand around the marooned sailor's leg. When the circle is complete, both sailors are free to run around again. The rescuer cannot be caught by the shark while he is drawing the circle.

The shark has won when all the sailors are marooned at the same time, and then a new shark is picked for the next game.

We also like to make a

little safe island. Dig a hole in the sand, just big enough for one person. This is a place where you can rest if you are getting tired. However, if someone else jumps in, then you must jump out, no matter how short a time you have been there!

If the shark is finding it too difficult, you can add a rule that once a sailor has been marooned and rescued, he is only allowed to hop on one leg.

NOUGHTS AND CROSSES

Find a patch of sandy beach, and draw a noughts-and-crosses grid in the sand. Then use stones for the noughts and shells as your crosses.

If you are on a pebbly beach, look for sticks, seaweed or driftwood to form the grid, and use only white pebbles perhaps for the crosses, and bits of found plastic for the noughts.

You may be able to find flat stones on which you can draw a grid using a chalky stone. Don't forget to try bumper versions using three-or four-lined grids, trying to score as many lines of three as you can.

THE AUTAN RANGE AT A GLANCE:

Autan offers you 2 skin repellent ranges and an after-bite spray. All Autan products are:

- Non-sticky and non-greasy
- Pleasant fresh fragranced
- Suitable for children over the age of 2 years
- Dermatologically tested

Autan Active Skin Repellent
- Strong protection for up to 8 hours
- Designed for outdoor endurance activities
- Available as a 100ml pump, 50ml stick or 100ml body spray

Autan Family Skin Repellent
- Strong protection for up to 4 hours
- Aloe Vera moisturises, cools and soothes the skin
- Available as a 100ml balm spray or 100ml and 200ml lotion

Autan Bite-Ease
If you forget to apply a repellent...
- Cools and soothes insect bites and stings
- Long lasting
- Special micropump makes it easy and hygienic to apply
- Handy 8ml spray

The Active range provides protection for up to 8 hours and the Family range for up to 4 hours. If you forget to apply a repellent, use Autan Bite-Ease to cool and soothe insect bites and stings.

Which Autan product is right for you?

	Up to 4 hours protection	Up to 8 hours protection	Insect bite relief
Adults Children over 2 years of age	AUTAN FAMILY	AUTAN ACTIVE	AUTAN BITE-EASE
Infants under 2 years of age	Avoid areas at risk, cover up with long sleeved clothing.		

NOTE ON THE AUTHORS

Suzy Barratt and Polly Beard are sisters. Suzy lives in Dorset with Joss, Elmo and Lola the dog. Polly lives in London with Tom, Ella and Jojo.

We'd love to know your favourite games or your comments and variations on the games in this book. Please visit our website: **www.imboredbooks.com**

A NOTE ON AUTAN

For more information, call us FREE:

Mon – Fri 8am to 6pm
0800 353 353
www.autan.co.uk

SC Johnson Ltd, Frimley Green, Camberley,
Surrey, GU16 7AJ
Autan® is a registered trademark of SC Johnson Ltd